SHAPESHIFTERS

# SHAPESHIFTERS

## DÉLANI VALIN

**NIGHTWOOD EDITIONS**

2022

Nightwood Editions
P.O. Box 1779
Gibsons, BC VON 1V0
Canada
www.nightwoodeditions.com

COVER DESIGN: Angela Yen
TYPOGRAPHY: Carleton Wilson

Nightwood Editions acknowledges the support of the Canada Council for the Arts, the
Government of Canada, and the Province of British Columbia through the BC Arts Council.

This book has been produced on paper certified by the FSC.

Printed and bound in Canada.

LIBRARY AND ARCHIVES CANADA CATALOGUING IN PUBLICATION

Title: Shapeshifters / Délani Valin.
Names: Valin, Délani, author.
Description: Poems.
Identifiers: Canadiana (print) 20220252254 | Canadiana (ebook) 20220252300 |
ISBN 9780889714281 (softcover) | ISBN 9780889714298 (EPUB)
Classification: LCC PS8643.A4265 S53 2022 | DDC C811/.6—dc23

*For Joseph:*
*May we continue to shift, grow.*

# CONTENTS

III

IV

I

## STARBUCKS

I used to sink southern ships
with the flick of a fin. Watched
old whaling captains lock
themselves in their chambers.
I followed the wrecks, swam
down to comfort sailors,
stroked their black-algae hair
as they succumbed to stillness.

The water warmed—
it scalded skin and scale.
Corals caved to acid. I found
the whales humming, high-pitched
like kettles. We swam
past rusting tankers spewing
waste, and garbage barges
trapping seagulls in plastic rings.

Tangled and squirming,
they hoisted me into harbour.
Held down, examined, probed,
I was brought to Pike Place
to become a fish-tossed mascot.

I sometimes stare at the sea
to look at the floating paper cups.

# BARBIE

The paparazzi says I shouldn't exist—
I'm a waifish waste of a woman
whose organs couldn't possibly fit
behind my ribs. They thought my silence
was suspicious. But back in my day
it wasn't chic to speak. Ken said,
"Hell, you're as big and bitchy
as any woman I've met."

They call him a silver fox now.
It's a masculine noun meaning
(usually divorcé) greying male
celebrity cast opposite
a woman under thirty.

And me? No silver in sight.
I bleach my roots every two weeks,
take the Botox shots between
the rhino- and labia-plasty. Some say
I look good for nearly sixty
(as long as I keep my convertible
top up and stay tucked, mouth
shut, in my dream house).

# MICHELIN MAN

Amidst the scent of gasoline, I soap and scour the inky smears from
　　this round body,
Cleanse oil, grease, curses—bitch hips, chick tits—clinging to this
　　spellbound body.

In a dream I was sanded down, polygonal and sharp as a fawn's
　　angled knee,
Insults from guys in the shop glanced off the tapered thighs of that
　　sound body.

God is a good night's sleep. God is the sun on my shoulders before I
　　shield them,
On the day the doctor refused me treatment, God was the rib of a
　　greyhound's body.

A sun radiates from my belly through rage, ulcer, through ragged
　　contempt,
Circular hatred, yet I'm no more my mind than my left toe in this
　　battleground body.

Open your mouth and say *sumptuous* when I thrust. Let me show
　　you my power,
I am Mars in furs—this is fullness: tenderness and force against
　　your unbound body.

I am the banquet of my being, Bibendum. Devoured at last by
　　embodied life,
Weight may wax, wane. But the moon of my belly is the altar of my
　　crowned body.

## MRS. CLEAN

Yes, he cooks! He cleans!
He writes grocery lists!
But oh, how low
the bar is set.
I should be lucky,
after all most men
aren't used
to scrubbing a toilet.

My husband's muscles
bulge against the cotton
of his skin-tight bleached
t-shirt. I'm told he's ideal
in every way. He won't touch me
without wearing his yellow rubber
gloves. Yet he plucks hairballs
with bare hands from the neighbour's
drain. Mops and dusts and who knows
what. I'll spike his club soda
with lemon and Clorox. Watch
his bald ass Magic Erase that.

# RONALD

Among the aspen leaves rusting in the sun, a western tanager builds a nest with the stiff fibres of a bright-red wig. A fox paws delicately through the brush to sniff at a yellow jumpsuit. An elk lifts a velvet tongue dipped in the milky waters of puddle and ivory paint. Sixteen bison stretch their necks and tear at grasses. One raises its head of rich matted fur, fixes his brown tourmaline eye on a man. A naked man kneeling, his soft genitals drooping, his arms hanging limp.

Echoless grunting
The now settles around them
Eyes, hooves, breath, no plan

## THE SEAL

some god is large enough
to hold us all.
that day in the harbour

two men
pulling up traps
raw chicken, brined. crabless.

and the seal:
eyes my curves,
the faux fur coat.

40 per cent off: bargain
hunter. clumsy on land,
i shuffle on the boardwalk.

seal swims up, then shiny
head submerges, i dive.
with coat, combat boots,

wallet with loyalty
cards. i bought the seal
a novelty hat:

*fish fear me,*
*my lover wants*
*to hold me*

by the neck. zookeeper
pushes balls to nose,
balls to nose and arch back.

i fumble the cap.
seal leads me through:
kelp gardens, molson

aluminum installations.
there is a school of rockfish
and seal roars, undulates.

i swim my fist and grasp:
slippery, struggling,
yellow fins fanning.

first bite: saline, soft,
squishy. fish eye swirls.
gills pulsate under finger.

they had it coming.
fangless and gushing,
deadpan. seal peers at me

through blood. isn't it
funny that we're held
all the same?

## BETTY CROCKER

I know what you're thinking
so go ahead:
indict me for carving myself into my kitchen,
impeach the blank calendar hanging
on my fridge. I closed my curtains years ago,
cut out my coupons, kept the chaos away
by keeping my family full

I did what I could, and I do what I can
with these standards I cannot stand: you want
quick/super-moist/easy
Now is that a woman or a cookie?

If the question bothers you
close the kitchen door
Crack the eggs, and find a chore

# THE GIANTESS

The day she stopped shrinking
her shoulders in the 99 B-Line bus seat,
she shot up fifteen hundred feet. Her head
tore through the roof of the bus.
She brushed metal debris
out of her hair—a mangled emergency
exit clattered to the asphalt. Pedestrians
scurried for shelter and cars fled like rats
between her thundering footsteps. Her boyfriend

clung to her white writhing shoelace.
He managed to hold on until
she noticed him screaming. She paused
at a playground and picked him up by the neck
of his H&M shirt. She set him on a swing
and flicked the seat. He soared skyward.
Finally, she'd made good on his request
to give him the ride of his life.

She trampled on through the city.
A blink of silk-ribbon lashes swept crows and gulls
from her eyes. She caught sight of the sea.

Running, she shook the maze of glass buildings
behind her. The water was cold but she didn't
hesitate to plunge in. Swam, capsized
ships with swells that swallowed the shore.
She smiled, spun onto her back. Floated.

She became a landmass,
grew forests on the convex curve of her belly.

## THE ESSENTIAL

Linda, I heard you get up and start the beef brisket. The meat
and gravy powder, ready by five. Do you ever think about time?

I don't mean how it slows down on the job. It's how you heat
your coffee thermos—that three-dollar Value Village vessel—

heat and reheat, with no moment to sit and sip. Or the loud tick
of your body clock guessing whether it's already first frost. People

at work are hungry for something all day, and later you notice the full
moon as you limp back to your truck. *Nice night,* you say. And Tammy

tells you to keep out of trouble and it also means, *Love you!* What
is essential? Coming home and caring for your mother who smiles

at cowboy-show reruns and cacti, feeding the cats, keeping coughs
to a minimum, or else the old remedies come out. Have you heard

how a garlic clove cures an earache? Who knows? Had a good day?
There are spaces within us that answer: back aches and blisters.

We are hired for our skills and we are hired for compulsory gratitude,
a smile of normalcy, steadfast cheerfulness—you're very welcome.

The forty-hour workweek was designed to have angelic housewives
concocting grocery lists and pot pies in the background. And now it's closer

to the nine-to-nine. Beep, beep, the brisket is tender, and there is always
someone new in line. Being a parent can be a thankless gig, and feeding

people and driving them around and delivering mail and teaching children
and reversing mortgages and treating sick dogs and harvesting lentils

and repairing the roads is thanked with Facebook posts, Pizza Fridays
and poems. Clock in, clock out. May you have more than a moment.

# THE DRYAD

They found her on Mr. Williams' lawn,
curled up on the crew-cut cropped grass,
above four inches of topsoil,
next to stainless-steel sprinklers.

His large greying t-shirt grazed
her velvet moss-whelmed thighs,
spindly burrs clung to ropey mats
in her cinnamon hair.
Her arms trellised ivy vines
entwined with pea plants—
their pods plump with pearls.

A crowd formed around her dirt-spangled body,
joggers stopped to see the rhizomes sprouting
from her feet. Children ditched their bicycles
on the side of the street. They watched her unfurl,
rise and open her eyelids—

Two succulents bloomed, unblinking,
like bulbous cabbages in the sunken
grooves above her nose. She fixed them
on her speechless company, held out a seed,
breathed, *Plant me a tree.*

# THE SHAPESHIFTER
*for Liam*

## I. PETER PARKER

Show me the origin
of your pain. Did you adopt it in childhood
when you were given the wrong name?
Was it hiding in every pleat
of every floral cotton dress?

The radioactive bite of chemicals
courses in your bloodstream. You say the needles don't stop
your feeling inept. You say what hurts
the most is scrolling down computer screens,
clicking through profiles of people
who type, *i like you, i like you, except…*?
You knew changing would be hard
But nobody warned you about the loneliness.

## II. LAZARUS

I watch you dig ever downward
in search of subterranean solace.
Maybe there will be romance
among the writhing white worms.
Kiss them, they are blind and jawless.
With them, you can forget.
What body? What name?
What anxious disassociating mess
of hyperventilating cold sweat?

Rise now. I followed you into the grave
and I am clawing at the dirt with broken fingernails.
I'm screaming your name. You may not believe
in your right to lift your chin, much less your right to live, but I would
    give anything to resurrect you.

Ten thousand rats have died for your medications.
I would kill ten thousand more to see you lift one eyelid and find the sun.

## III. Dr. Manhattan

I am not religious but I prayed for your ascent. Now
before me you stand taller than you've ever been.
Blue and built superhuman, supermachine.
We both know you're omnipotent, a giant striding
through the neighbourhoods that forced you
to be complacent. Recognize your transformation,
hold me in your palm. I trust you.
Do you finally trust you are enough?

# THE GEOLOGIST

*while now she laments her acne*

We scorn the Earth
for its topography.
Map, drill, mine. Catalogue
findings and assign value.
Gold, emerald, hematite

*her fetishized features*

shimmer under scrutiny.
With enough pressure
perhaps every element
becomes a diamond.
Shrinks smaller,

*and the space she takes*

becomes a speck of glittering
dust. Yet below the surface,
resistance ripples.
Tectonic restlessness
threatens change:

*she will soon understand*

there will be more
than shaken-loose gravel,
more than a disturbance
of sand. Think of a subterranean
collision, a crumbling cliff,

*there is power beyond*

an open fault, a disappearing
island. A tsunami flooding
a forest, far above the shoreline.
We'll abandon our tools
and run. We won't have

*control over the shape of her body,*

our mundane worries, agony
over choosing a cereal brand,
empty New Year's resolutions.
We'll grab for solid ground
through handfuls of sediments

*there is power in a fistful of dirt*

when we have nothing else.
After we regain our footing,
slump over to the stillest
water we can find, we'll see
our own scowls mirrored

*thrown back into hateful faces.*

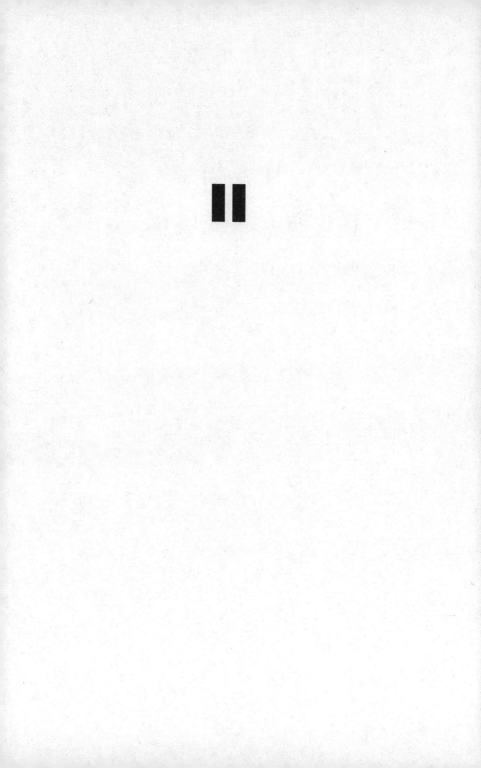

## DEAR GREGOR SAMSA

I hope it wasn't insensitive to bring
you a garden snail in our wretched states.
See it in its terrarium, stomach foot and shell,
how graceful it paints the glass with slime.
We skitter to your room. I remind you I'm here

at great risk to myself. I'm covered in scarves
but there are parts of me I can't hide.
The snail stretches its tentacles—
slow radial twirls, eye stalks scanning
moss and twig, unseeing my monstrous
shape. I place the glass box by your bedside
and I fill you in: Britney Spears
is free at last. They're still making
fried chicken sandwiches with
fried chicken buns, et cetera. I shiver
when you brush against my thorax—
grotesque rippling of skeleton and skin.
*It's getting late,* I say. It's nearly dawn and
the snails will be out for their morning meals,
my neighbours will soon be gathering
in the lobby to make eye contact and chatter.
*It's been good.* I unfurl my legs beneath me—
tarsi and tibiae waterlogged from rain
and ragged. I haven't looked at yours and I won't.
You croak, *Do you still love me?* I tell you the snail
likes its shell gently scrubbed with a toothbrush.
I tell you the snail is partial to apple, cucumber,
mushroom, boiled and cooled carrots.
I tell you what else is palatable.

# NO BUFFALOS

*for Connie*

I

I'm capital-M Métis. The proof:
official cards, forms, anatomy.
High cheekbones, dark hair, Red
River veins—sanctioned subcutaneous

topography. Is there an ideal?
It's not me: I called my mother's
mother Grandma, not Nohkom.
And she told me of being cold

in Meadow Lake, school lunches
clanging frozen in tin pails, sharing
shabby rooms with brothers,
praying and growing up motherless.

What about our history? I glimpsed
it in fifth grade. PowerPoint
presentations of figure-eight flags, fiddles—
men shot and hanged. Couldn't identify

with violent static slides. Instead
I memorized names like Dumont and Riel.
Got the grades, let go of the sash
and the scrip. Moved on, Batoche blip.

II

When Grandpa was alive, he rented
a modest double-wide in a trailer park
off a hustler-held, crime-lined
highway. He filled glass dishes

with candy for our visits. Grandma cooked
stew in the bleached-white kitchen. Cousins
in the living room compared each other's
features. Who's pretty? Who's *Indian*?

*She's got Native cheeks.* I flattened them
with clammy palms. Slathered on
the makeup, Fair, Pearl, Porcelain. Bullies
in high school taught me Cree was still there.

Ethnicity checklists assured constant
presence of well-meaning, white education assistants.
*You're Métis? You need a tutor.*
*You're struggling. You're distant.* I was

reconciling my awkward appearance
with pictures of smooth-faced ancestors.
At last I let the sun pick a tint and daydreamed
of embedding beaded flowers in my skin.

III

I rented a room in a dank Vancouver
basement: iron bars on tiny window,
narrow twin bed, perpetually dirty
dishes, gloom-mute roommates

too morose to speak. The landlord, film-
school professor, lived upstairs: *No talking*
*after eight, no guests, no burning—what is that,*
*sage?* I smoked a thick Romeo y Julieta

on the eve I moved away. Crossed the country
with my boyfriend, leased a Montreal
apartment. Exchanged English pleasantries
and French profanities with my neighbour—

a fist-bumping septuagenarian who claimed
he drank whole cans of maple syrup straight.
Rats and roaches skittered in our kitchen.
Câlisse! Calvaire! I've never lived on grassy

plains. Carpets of canola, dollops of clouds
in a too-vast sky: prairie provinces are an ellipses
connecting the concrete cores I've called home. Where
I live, tall glass buildings shape the days. There are no buffalos.

IV

Styrofoam packs and blood pads,
plastic wrap pulled against refrigerated
flesh: pre-seasoned, dismembered
pigs glisten. I'm standing on the edge

of the aisle, far from the abattoir
where workers dunk still-alive swine
in vats of boiling water to shed hair
from their skin. We do away with the eyes.

Stroking the beaver-tuft trim
on moose-hide moccasins gives me visions
of my own skin slathered in my brains,
stretched in the sun. Muscles wound

into sticky sinew. Liver wrapped
in parchment paper and tossed
into a freezer. There are no
gentle bullets. The only blood

I drink drips from blackberries
picked behind seedy strip malls. I eat
soup with corn, squash, beans.
Vegetables are easier to mourn.

v

June outside the hospital pavilion:
someone funded a new wing. We're dancers
on demand: we Métis and a group of First
Nations people from Cowichan.

I'm twelve. Wearing a choker, bright-
red skirt over crinoline, a garter
grown-up enough to make up for
misgivings about pigtail braids that frame

my too-round face. Best friend's a blonde Mi'kmaq
girl who wasn't the *right* kind of Métis
for an official card, but good enough to dance.
We hold hands, demonstrate "The Red River Jig,"

"Drops of Brandy," "Rabbit Dance." Shuffle
through the steps, hear the instructor
joke—*It's Métis cardio!*—as she invites
the clappers in the crowd to join us.

A Cowichan boy cuts in, stumbles,
shouts over the fiddle. I accept
the compliment, cough, thank
exertion for masking blush.

VI

I feel guilty about struggling
with my duality. Hungry for
stereotypical narratives of helpful
Cree women voluntarily teaching

European men to survive the freezing
plains. How old were my mothers
when they were wed? I can't
reconcile the cavalier, colonial

manifest destiny of male ancestors
with my hypersensitivity. Was I born
out of violence? Ask Kisemanito
or count beads on the rosary.

*Get over it*, says the anonymous
internet commenter on the CBC.
Should we forget road allowance,
Rooster Town, getting by on roasted

gopher meat? I won't make peace
with the past. Can't bifurcate
my history. I can only collect
my Elders' memories and write.

I was in a French program in high
school. We used government funding
for a field trip to Saskatchewan. Toured
tiny St. Denis, population thirty.

My friend and I were restless,
bored with teachers' authority. We ran down
a dirt road, past a buffalo ranch, through
a grove of twisted trees. We rested in an

abandoned farmhouse full of porcelain
cups and calendars. Respite from the buzz:
mosquitos and too-chatty classmates.
Almost missed the bus to Batoche.

Neon-green grass, bullet-pocked white church.
I imagined what my ancestors might
have copped to in confessional. Was it worse
than running away on field trips and stealing

cigarettes? In the cemetery I stared at my great-
great-uncle's grave. Later, my mother opened
a textbook about Métis history, showed me a picture
of his gunned-down corpse. *Donald Ross. Say his name.*

VIII

I take my medicine. As a child I used chicken soup,
fizzy ginger ale, saccharine bubble-gum syrup.
Now, I swallow Ativan, Klonopin, Effexor chemical
compounds that keep me from death by shallow

breath. I've been reading what my ancestors
have known for centuries: the benefits of rat root,
rosehips, seneca, sage. Harvesting rhizomes, stems
and leaves to treat colds, coughs, pain. How to use

sweetgrass to focus nervous energy, how to decoct
nettles for tea. Is there a benefit to sharing this knowledge?
Respect for Indigenous people and land? Downtown Montreal
in an Urban Outfitters, there are cellophane bags

stapled shut, labelled *Spirit Sage*. Sold alongside mass-
manufactured Ojibwe-inspired dreamcatchers, Navajo prints,
two-hundred-dollar tipi tapestries. All things here are trendy:
the astrological ashtrays, the tongue-in-cheek cookbooks

for grilled cheese. Fashion distills meaning, and fades. Cute
feathered artifacts and moccasins made in China are not
as authentic as rubber bullets, tear gas and the cancers
borne out of degraded environments. What's the medicine for that?

Mother grew up in the North. Hay
River: small town, big family. She drew
strength from the *lap, lap, lap* of the Great
Slave Lake. Went to school, learned

her vocabulary: rebellion, Riel, halfbreed,
treason. Little reason to acknowledge
ancestry when textbooks dissect all
the ways you've been beaten. She was forty

when she circled back to map her genealogy.
Applied for her card, got a job teaching
Métis culture and history. Brought birchbark
and beads to class, brought buckskin

jackets and sashes home. Enlisted me
to dance, said, *Maybe not now, but one day*
*this inheritance will make you proud.* Yet,
like me she's questioned on authenticity

by our own community: *You don't have* lived
*Métis experience.* What counts and who decides?
We all have stories, we're all legitimate. Don't
believe otherwise, Mama, that's bisonshit.

x

I'm a product of my generation:
put too much faith in post-modern
pastiche collages of my culture. Here
is a glass bead I sewed onto an Old

Navy sweater, a fake feather I glued
to a mood board. A Michif word
sprinkled for flavour, a quick smudge
of sage when I'm stressed, a mini sash

in the back of my closet, my heirlooms
and modern trinkets coalesce. I want
to adapt without assimilating, but maybe
I'm kidding myself. With my five-dollar

soy lattes, credit cards and Halloween
costumes for dogs, I'm shoulder-deep
in colonial capitalism. In the Great Bear
Rainforest surrounded by giant cedars,

I struggle for words. I fear the violence
of pipelines, and other warped definitions
of progress. Is it possible to change *and* protect?
Ancestors say I should never fear a good fight.

# WHAT ARE THE ETHICS OF PICKING A STINGING PLANT?

I've been daydreaming of nettle. The underside of a flat leaf foaming with formic acid, little barbs licking wind. I've never harvested it before, but I think about bringing my scissors down to the lake. I wouldn't lay tobacco down like I'm supposed to, because I'd need to rip open a du Maurier and scatter the arsenic. That's bad medicine, I think. Bad ethics. I have black tea instead. I don't have access to pure tobacco here, is that okay? I daydream of just taking the top three inches from ten or twelve plants.

I'm sleepwalking. It's the smell of hot soup wafting from the lake, leading me. Tadpole and lily pad and skunkweed stew, or is Campbell's? I'm cooking up a way to wake up from this, but in the meantime, I tucked teal rubber gloves into my sweatshirt pocket. I felt real peace last summer when I filled bags with blackberries to burst. But neither fruit nor thorn know my name on this land, so I haunt their patches like a ghost.

The problem is that I'm a stranger to myself. And so, when Nettle asks, *Where are you from and who is your grandmother?* I can answer. It's all in the documents at home. It's all there in case you need proof. But when Nettle lowers their voice and asks, *Okay and who are you?* I think about my sadness and my credentials and a story I made up when I was seven. I say something like, *I'm just trying to be here.*

Nettle looks, and sees. *Soup's on,* they say. They mean nettle minestrone. They mean I am also in the broth. So when I wake up one day, my hands will still be stinging.

# TERRARIUM

Inhale ire and exhale worry. Hotbox your bachelor suite, pray
over holy basil chamomile concoctions for the frazzled

rhizomes of your sympathetic nerves. Bury the bones
of the animals you wish you didn't need to eat.

Medicate: rum, milk thistle, rum, repeat. Pack the wounds
with mud and try to carry on. I come in with a shovel

but I also carry the hum of a million mundane car rides,
I'm asthmatic, with jagged gravel specks embedded in my feet, pollution,

my bleak, dogged atheism. Cleanse me. And I will help you
tie the twined, dried lemon balm and lavender from the ceiling. Sow

a row of carrots in your bedsheets. Sneak in all of the endangered
arbutuses and oaks. Plant little succulents in the countertops, and feed

honey to the moss spreading across the shower walls. Filtered
water for the willows, and coffee grounds for the fig trees. Lay with me

on the dirt-covered linoleum and place your pomegranate seeds
on my tongue. Let's turn this soil together. Look how good, how grounded.

# TELOGEN EFFLUVIUM

*for Claude*

## Centre Gather

I'm safe on Vancouver Island. I'm safe. Except my shoulders scrape my earlobes and my hands look like little claws that I shake out. That I ball up and shake out.

I'm safe. I'm standing in the room I rent from my friend's parents. The bed is comfortable, my suitcases piled on the ground with clothes spilling out. Most of them still smell of a specific cologne. Expensive. Acrid.

Shake it out. I'm trying to practise this new skill called "self-soothe." There are a lot of ways to go about this, I'm told by therapists and by the kind woman at the Victim Services office. *None of this is your fault,* she'd said over and over. Experience taught her this was something I needed to hear. Experience taught her that I didn't quite believe it.

The therapist gave me printouts. One with a long list of self-soothing activities such as: *Go for a walk, Call a friend, Make a warm cup of tea.* My eyes dart to number fifty-six, which says, *Brush your hair.* For days I've been avoiding my boar-bristle brush still tucked in my suitcase because lately whenever I comb my hair, so many strands loop around the bristles and clump into big tufts. Then I pull the tufts out and throw them in the plastic grocery garbage bag on my bedroom floor. This is normal, after trauma. You can lose hair for about three months. Braiding is better than brushing. Weaving keeps things intact, and distracts from what happened. What happened?

## STRAND

Before colonization, Coast Salish peoples used fur from dogs to weave wool blankets. I learned this fact a decade ago from my friend Jesse, who learned it from the knowledge-keepers in his community. Two years ago, researchers at last examined the fibres from a blanket in Seattle and found hairs from that now extinct, tiny, woolly breed of dog. Hard proof. This is what it takes to validate oral stories, right? This is what it takes to be believed.

## STRAND

I walk a lot. I walk all of the kilometres that I couldn't when I was back there. I walk to show myself that between fight, flight, freeze or fawn, I can still choose flight instead of fawn.

I walk on bike paths between groaning highways and desolate train tracks. Overgrowth of weeds and wildflowers feed the bees. I spot a lavender bush and stay my grasping hand from plucking at it. I am not someone who tries to possess what is beautiful and alive.

When I was in Cotonou, my family, by marriage, wanted to share everything. So generous: their offerings of *sauce arachide*, their dance lessons at weddings, their protectiveness when I bartered in markets for beautiful necklaces. They brought me to a hair studio so I could try out a new style.

It was a week before the Christmas holidays, which was strange because of the sunshine and beaches and slender black Santas. Little girls slept in chairs while dexterous women braided their hair into beautiful cornrows and Senegalese twists. I was the only white-coded person in the salon. The assumption was that I was French, and not the usual guesswork quilt I copped in Canada: one day Lebanese, one day Latina, one day *ethnic of some sort*. Never Métis.

The woman who sat me in her styling chair pursed her lips at the sight of me. She brushed my fine hair. It was greasy. It was flat. The woman looked at me like she was sorry for my situation. But I was the one who apologized for the texture of my hair that slipped between her fingers as she laboured to make the tiny braids needed to sew in my weave. Perhaps those long Brazilian wefts would make me look beautiful and alive. Maybe I would have more confidence, like the women on this side of my family. They always seemed to be able to say no.

STRAND

Arbutuses are evergreen trees that often grow on rocky cliffs near the ocean. They withstand strong winds and droughts, their trunks and branches grow scraggly, adapting to the challenges. They're a food source for hummingbirds. Woodpeckers and robins pluck their berries. Their bark, traditionally used for medicine, sheds like paper scrolls, leaving smooth red trunks that adolescents tend to plunge their pocket knives into to carve their current crushes' initials. The trees are in decline. Climate stress leaves them more susceptible to blight—black spots appear on their leaves and the stress and illness leads to defoliation.

STRAND

I chewed on my hair on the plane ride back from Cotonou. I already missed the sunshine and the songs, the hugs and the laughter. But getting treatment and therapy would be easier back home.

I had too much to drink courtesy of Air France, and the woman sitting beside me matched my pace, champagne for champagne. We had both boarded in Paris. She was Indian and wore her long, thick hair plaited down her back. Over the hum of the engine she told me her terrible story. I told her mine. Eerily similar. Ears popped, like I couldn't believe what I was hearing. She smoothed my hair and we cried.

STRAND

Your hair conditioner may contain sheep's sebum. But it's good for the hair. Sheep are shorn, their wool scoured, and the oily substance collected from the scouring waters is called wool grease. This is refined into a product called lanolin, and when essential oils and preservatives are added, it completely masks the foul smell.

STRAND

When I confessed to my generous family what happened, it was too much. I repeated the play-by-play and received feedback. Did they believe me?

Did they believe me? I visualized tearing my hair out in patchy clumps. Maybe I made it so real that my follicles simply surrendered the strands for the next three months. *We just need to know the full story.* Okay, here it is.

## STRAND

Wait—here's a recipe for a hair mask I use to make my hair nice and shiny! The peppermint is stimulating and brings blood flow to the scalp, which helps promote hair growth.

Ingredients:
½ ripe avocado
1 Tbsp of honey
1 Tbsp of coconut oil
2 drops of peppermint essential oil

## METHOD

Melt the coconut oil and honey together in a small saucepan. Meanwhile, mash the avocado in a bowl. Add the coconut oil and honey to the avocado, and squeeze in the essential oil. Apply mask to hair, and leave on for twenty minutes. Rinse well, and shampoo and conditioner as normal.

Anyway, twenty Christmases before the one I spent in Cotonou, my mom turned on those classic kids' cartoons: Charlie Brown and Linus on a mission to find a Christmas tree. The tree they chose was pathetic, losing its needles, and Lucy got on their case for choosing something so ugly. But Linus wrapped his blanket around the trunk and they accepted the little tree.

My parents took turns brushing my bangs back from my forehead at night. My dad told me my favourite bedtime story about a freezing marmot that dug through the earth from snowy Quebec City to the warmth of Mexico. It would have shed its winter coat to sunbathe on the sunny beaches, safe. I believed it all.

## TACIT

There are no safe spaces
There never were—our mothers
whispered their woes
to the wainscotting, washed
a dull spotless white

We're tired—there's no end
to the leering in the streets, no
matter whether we shroud
our bodies, speak dulcet thanks, hiss
Whether we meet those thirsting eyes
(blue, brown, hazel, green—any
remind us to shrink
into obedience)

Join me in the periphery,
hide in the forgotten harbours
on the fringes of reality—

Picnics on the yellowed grass bordering
transnational highways
Night jogs on still-warm airport runways
Naps in the elevator shaft just beyond the boardroom

Come and fade from the endless grasping
The compliments
            the catcalls
                the vi
                            ol
                                en
                        c
                        e

# HUNGER

My kid sister is an aspiring bodybuilder. She adores the fitness model shapeshifters in *Natural Muscle* and *Flex*. She eats Cliff bars, curbs dairy, counts calories and considers taking creatine. But at least she eats, instead of starving for survival, scaling her way to some scant little after party, for which the guest list grows sparser by the second. I stood there once. The food was terrible.

I was told I must have done it for attention. The luna moth, *Actias Luna*, did it for sex, but I did not. The luna moth larva eats leaves of walnut, hickory and sumac. After moulting, it emerges with a wingspan of four-and-a-half inches. Its wings are green like the foliage on which it had fed. However, it no longer eats. As an adult, the luna moth is mouthless. It starves to death, living only for a week. Its sole purpose: to procreate.

The squirming organs under my skin eventually win. Amino acids and lipids and polysaccharides enter the esophagus. At this point, the saliva's enzyme, amylase, has already begun disintegrating the starch. It is microscopic.

My mother used to tell me stories before bed. She said to beware the Rugarus—large furry creatures that ate any living thing including Métis children who get out of bed too many times, and their mothers, too. She said they mostly live near the Red River, but if they're hungry enough who knows how far they'll travel? She told me: *If you see a Rugaru, you become one straight away, because that sort of hunger is contagious.*

# TEETH

They chant, *We'll crumble out of your face and you'll have no one*
*but yourself to blame.* They sing to me in my dreams—dramatis personae:
Molars, Incisors, Cuspids, Bicuspids, Canines. I ache
like it's the 1920s, like I'm a Radium Girl:
point my radioactive paintbrush with pursed lips.
Swallow my luminous saliva that eats through veneers.

Beyond that bullshit Coke Zero pumped steady
through these aspartame-rich veins, or shots
of apple cider vinegar that amateur nutritionists promise
will make me thin.
I don't brush when I'm depressed:
easier to deny being in this body and embody negligence.
Can't face the mirror no matter how shower-fogged, I can't
face those dull yellowing bones. I chew Tic Tacs all day
for the benefit of the Walmart greeter who waves
while I pick up my Prozac. It causes cotton-mouth, and dryness
accelerates tooth decay. If I need a filling
just let it be sweet.

# HYPOCHONDRIA

It's worse when I'm under a lot of stress.
Sit up in bed. Scratch my dry, over-washed hands,
shove them in my lap. Gym shorts—today I'll run,
pick up barbells, drink two litres of water.
Toned hamstrings and a glow indicate health,
endorphins give me perspective. Reframe, reset.

Chest pain at work. Is it pneumonia? Lung cancer? No, reset.
Cashier coworker is coughing, too—a cold. Don't stress.
Buy the white bottles in the supplement section labelled health,
chew vitamin C tablets and echinacea. Sanitize hands.
Throw away the coworker-contaminated bottle of water.
We close at eleven. Will I still have time to run?

Power on my Mac. Log consumed calories, log my seventeen-kilometre run,
log sleep, log any strange symptoms. Computer crash. Reset.
Now ten in the morning and I'm exhausted. Caffeine crash. Drink water.
Make appointment with therapist. *Have you been feeling any stress?*
I think I'm fine. Work's good. Workout's good. I wring my hands.
*Meditate on "holistic": we want spiritual, physical and mental health.*

As if I'm not constantly thinking about my health?
I tell her about the weird pain in my gut. She nods. I want to run
out of her office. Settle for slouching. Cradle my head in my hands.
*I get it—you need more rest. Take a vacation from work, and reset.*
I just want a break from my head. Squeeze my knuckles. They crack
    under stress.
She talks coping skills: *When it's bad, splash yourself with cold water.*

I shower as soon as I'm home. Linger under running water.
Soap, shampoo, conditioner. Is this hair falling out a sign of poor health?
Could be anemia, low protein or lupus? A doctor might say that it's stress.
Panic mounts nonetheless. I stumble into leggings and sneakers and run.
Chemical reactions in my brain. I can breathe better now. Reset.
Calm in my mind, calm in my body. No more tight chest, no tingling hands.

I trip on the pavement. Catch myself on the palms of my hands.
Skin torn, bleeding. Embedded with dirt. Yell for water
to rinse myself off. A man on a bike ignores me. I try again. Reset.
Shout about bacterial infections and risks to my health.
He cycles on. My ankle hurts—it's sprained or broken. Can't run.
Pull out my cellphone. Does tripping on asphalt count as dis-stress?

Clasp my phone in my hands. The screen resists breaking under stress.
I resist, too. Pull up a video of a river—whitewater—I watch it run.
Scrapes can be washed, bones can be reset. Repeat the mantra: *I'm in
good health.*

# WELLNESS

To whom do we turn, we intractable malcontents—sip-sick
on whisky or the brew of our own bloodstreams. Undiagnosed,

darting from doctor to doctor. *Knock, knock* in a new office,
another workup to do. I'm here for sadness and for the flapping

of my hands when I'm scared, and the way the sun glints off
rooftop barbwire like childhood cheekbone glitter, and the fluff

white marshmallow dog that heeds his toddler before lapping at the lake,
the light frames that emanate from apartment windows, each square

expressing a resident's particulars—glaring white bulbs and microwaved
meatloaf before sleep, blue flashing rerunned Lenos and Lettermans
       and minty

melatonins under tongues. The orange glow of dimmer-switch dining room
chandeliers presiding over tabletop family game nights—gather round,

and see how healthy I am in my wrongness, how many hereditary disorders
declared then dismissed, as I calmly waver on my will to live. Every new pill

a wager on whether nausea and joint pain and headaches caused by sentient
weed whackers haunting my neighbourhood will be worse than what
       plagues me.

Is it any wonder why we turn ourselves over to the altar of wellness? Swap
white coat for green juices. The celery and spirulina hollow out my
       hydro bill.

*Use your cookie budget for organic strawberries*, says my naturopath,
who has misinterpreted my fatness for mindless misinformation. Cookies

haven't graced my cupboards since indigestion, yet they're a more reliable
     tonic
than Gwyneth Paltrow's vagina-scented candles and an Oprah-sanctioned

soundbath. My prescription involves getting a better sleep and four hundred
dollars worth of vitamins, a waltz through a crystal emporium, charcoal
     smoothies

and a ceremony seemingly swiped from an ancestor's dance. I scrape
     and borrow
for seminars in which middle-class white women rock out and re-wild

and implore me to connect with an inner child that smudges sage imported
from endangered shrubs in Southern California. Hands pass over my back

to centre my energetic field and the tea-leaf reader tells me I will one
     day die,
the lazy certainty of Assam settling in porcelain cup. Cured cancer and
     Crohn's

testimonials plaster a website for a master class on breathing, as a
     chiropractor
unveils the quantum mechanics that fix quadriplegia, for a fee. A rose
     petal yoni

steam might not combat chlamydia, but it could release toxins to reveal
an inner goddess with good humour and a more robust immunity.
     Conspiracy

theories proliferate: perhaps my issues stem from that polio vaccine,
    or a deficiency
in coffee enemas, alkalized blood and hemp bedsheets. The yoga
    studio sighs

an empty *Namaste* while it sells pickle-juice gut-shots. What is wellness
when what's valued is the wheat stalk standing to golden attention,
    relentlessly

productive, ignoring its seasons unless going on a paid-for, team-
    building retreat?
I pace the carpet in my bedroom as I contemplate the prescriptions
    of Ritalin

and Ativan stacked with B vitamins and zinc on top of my fridge.
    Caught between
paradigms—they overlap in their cost and disconnection. And what's
    wrong? Seven

disorders, weak boundaries and doubt. The sun pearls a thousand water
    drops
from a malamute's back, his child-master's laughter spirals into puberty
    and crackles

in old age. Apartment tenants trade up to houses and down to suites,
    the cupboards
exchange one sentimental mug for another. My face ages and my body
    rounds.

My aloe vera sprouts a new shoot. Green, living and fragile. What is
    there to fix?

# HYMN

This sorceress sings over your cirrhosis. *Sweet*
*liver, let him purge the poison again.* Show me
your wounds and I will make you a poultice.
Show me a tear and I will steady your palm—
let it run. We must allow the water
to carve the Way. I drop
the Ten Thousand Things to see your eyes
crease when you greet me. You want connection:
we are two children on the edge of war-filled pasts.
Sleeping in a ditch, fumbling with Band-Aids
and bits of thread. I only have my hand to offer, and a chant—
*I am here, I am here.* You answer: *Until you aren't.*
You hide and I immolate myself.
I want to keep us warm, but my survival mechanisms
are no longer logical: I bite my own fingers.
You flinch at sustenance. As if every open hand
is marked with the neon tell of a scorpion.
Where's the venom? Where's the venom?
You even shrink from your reflection. But listen,
you have always been beautiful. Little boy who couldn't
count on Mom or Dad not doing the same old, same old
disappearing acts. I see you.
Later you're overweight and alone. But beauty
has never been perfect. I want to kiss your thighs—
stay still. There is no punchline. I'm a witch
with supernatural patience: test me.
Please don't fear my gifts, these little hits
of dopamine—pleasure doesn't always give way to punishment.
It's not all supposed to hurt. But when it does, and when it doesn't—
    I am here.

# DIAGNOSTIC CRITERIA 299.00

A

I speak to the moon through the fur of a senior wolfdog,
patting in flat circles, mapping the craters
behind the neck bones: axis, atlas. Moon answers
through the chipped cleft in a serving bowl.
Exposed, pocked grey ceramic above the apples.

Does this hollow have an ache for what it was?
Today I will attend a meeting to address timelines.
I will scoop out my powers, I will sit on my hands.
Until then I sympathize with broken dish, setting
satellite, sickening dog. For a time, Tuesdayless.

B

I collect simple spells, scatter them for friends like birdseed.
Do geese see God? We laugh at palindromes, portmanteaus.

I catalogue the laughter. Sophie and I share a strong appletini:
giggle. Joe sees my dewed face after the cat sneezes: guffaw.

C

As a child I befriended beetles and butterflies. At night,
I tried to take up with the imaginary critters my parents
created to keep me in bed by offering a handful of cereal.

I befriended a boy with a broomstick who said he'd beat me.
One summer we ate crushed dried ramen, licking chicken
powder from our fingers. His one black eye listed left
as he stole my ½ Lune cake. He told me I wasn't that bad.

D

*You are the god of this microcosm,* the mould of my teacup
titters in spores. I shake on the raft of my bed, adrift
in dust mites. Bills, errands, demands nip at my box spring.
The lighthouse cannot be trusted, it beacons memories
of winedrunk razorblade bites—past searches for shore.
Better to wait, and I'll be here for days. High-functioning.

E

I speak to the moon because it is framed as deficient relative to the sun.
I am deemed deficient relative to this orbiting mask:
*It's like Melanie with a D.* Smile. Eye contact.
Smile. Eye contact.
Smile. Eye contact.

# CARTILAGE

*My personal poetry is a failure.*

*I do not want to be a person.*

*I want to be unbearable.*

*Lover to lover, the greenness of love.*

—Anne Carson, "Stanzas, Sexes, Seductions"

The year I stopped craving strangers,
my right talus crumbled in my sock.
I made coasters with the X-rays.
They scooped out the bone.
I crawled around my mother's house,
losing pens and hair ties. I could be
a tulpa someone grew tired of,
each word spoken a conjured echo.
*My personal poetry is a failure.*

> I fare better at piercing barks.
> Dog and I yap at gulls and crows.
> A pair of bitches, her spayed.
> Dinner is meat and carrots we eat
> with tender mouths, disinclined and sore.
> Curl up in a bed that reeks of artificial pine.
> I ask her what it feels like to be female
> in her fur-covered body.
> *I do not want to be a person.*

> I want to be a god. But even
> Hecate is pinned to the crossroads:
> Maiden, mother, crone. Caverns, bone.
> Through gardens replete with garlic bulbs
> I snake, joints popping, searching for sky.

I spend the day in dirt. For the filthy
summer dress I am forgiven. For the soft
lisp in my singing voice, I am adored.
*I want to be unbearable.*

I am hungry for erosion. Three
years ago, Hecate greeted the null
animal of my dog. All smells
and smelling, nose to ground,
nose to open sky, I sense an ossuary:
the meaning of my hip bones.
Joints articulate, pain, pain-free, pain.
I trace the skin with blank fingertips.
*Lover to lover, the greenness of love.*

# MAGIC LESSONS

### I. TIME TRAVEL

I cry every time during takeoff—the no-escape of it. The surrender
to pilots, mechanics, God. I'm small. Telemetry brings our flight
over the ivory shores of Iceland—your ghost and I. It isn't that you're dead.

It's my codependent tendencies that drag you to the spaces in which I
    contract—
the lavatory, the inch separating my elbow from that stranger, the dark
between my thighs. Cavern, like the ones below where the Huldufólk dance

by little licks of firelight, while we sit up stiff in the sky for the fifth hour.
When we land in France (your spirit stuffed in my carry-on, never far),
we find there's sun where there shouldn't be. So I sleep

to release the ticks of Canadian hours still lodged in my marrow.
It takes a week. Between dreams I introduce you to family—
young cousins with box-braids, aunts in fur coats, the vulture.

A sluggish ride on the Metro to Montmartre sends me to expert,
sexist street tyrants trying to tie bits of string to my wrist for money. I pull
    away.
In the cheapest café I override my constant body shame long enough to bite

into the soft crust of a croissant. *Le Petit Prince* postcard and pen in hand—
I freeze time for evidence that I've thought of you here. I'm thinking of
    you now.
Bring you to all of the typical sites—Eiffel, Arc, Catacombs. I lick my teeth

at the sight of the bones. I send you videos of the worst Parisian riots
   since 1968.
Look at the water cannons. Look at the tear-gas stratus burning my eyes.
   I'm brave enough
to stand sentinel if your ghost doesn't drift back to your waking body.

## II. POTIONS

Come, little Casper. It's been a month since I left. Your faint and fair mist
    follows. Cover me—
I whisper to you in every unfamiliar situation. There are many.
I repeat, I repeat—we're in Africa. A mantra. The two hundred and forty
    inches

of my intestines struggle to process anything that isn't bottled water, and
    anti-malarials
mask hunger. Still, the cook comes in daily with sacks of spices, pouches
    of pepper,
shrimp powder. *Comme un renard et son Prince,* the cook and I tame

each other until I learn to trust his cuts of meat. He learns he can complain
    to me.
Like a fox, I tamed you too. Back in British Columbia, I passed the cooking
    quizzes
you solicited: the tenderness of boiled carrots, the lack of dairy. A checklist—

methods and ingredients brought on by distressing illness. I met the
    alchemy
of your hunger (your body transmutes chewed rice into golden energy)
    with bright
squeezed lemon and whispers of love to the poultry and poached greens.
    In turn

you taught me gratitude. A great cavalcade of thank yous to plants, animals,
farmers, soil, sunshine. It was the first time I prayed since fourth grade.
An agama skitters up the Cotonou kitchen walls. The cook asks if I've eaten

amiwo, then soaks plate and cutlery. Later, I hold his infant son. *Click*—
I freeze time for evidence that I've thought about you here. I'm thinking
 of you now.
There's photographic proof of my transgression. Disrespecting family's
 honour


by hugging too far down the hierarchy. I don't understand—the things
 I do for you,
I do for free. In this country I'm closer to cooks, chauffeurs, domestics
 and guards
than I should be. I can't tell love from labour. Everyone is so skilled in
 their trades.

## III. Divination

During the summer on Vancouver Island I shudder on my knees in a
    living room
filled with foam mattresses. Drink a glass of sticky brown Amazonian
    liquid. Bow—
you taught me gratitude. A great cavalcade of thank yous to plants,
    animals,

the god you talked about. Not the one I grew up with, all hypocritical
    holy men
and *Kill the Indian*. This one asks for nothing but to be felt. Psychedelic
    thought-
loops crest in the third hour. *Drum.* You're not the one. *Drum.* Even now,
    it's done.

I resist and stumble to the bathroom. On the toilet we're all equal—
    here is my
curved spine. My shivering, naked legs. Here is the violence of my acrid
    purple bile.
We all pray for the passing of a stomach cramp—pang born of illness,
    pang born

of shame. I come home to myself at five in the morning and call you
    with fresh,
loving denial. In Cotonou I ride shotgun with the chauffeur toward
    my initiation
at the voodoo convent. Stepmom, aunt, grandmother and vulture pile
    in the back.

In a small temple I eat cola nuts and watch a chicken's throat get slit
  for sacrifice.
*Ago, ago, ago:* apprentice knocks at the altar with spherical rock and
  dots clay
on my face, so that a high priest can say you're angry. I'm the one full
  of resentment.

Counting up my unmet needs. If I love you enough will it come back
  to me?
I freeze time for evidence that I've thought about you here. I'm thinking
  of you now.
Especially during a dalliance with a family friend—desperate attempt
  at connection.

I watch meek, good-girl self-belief shudder with new complexity and
  call you.
I brace myself for judgment. Stomach gurgles to digest shame. I
  hyperventilate.
But our rupture is full of grace. You break it off. Phantom turns poltergeist.

## IV. Spellwork

We agree not to speak. An emaciated, sand-coloured horse escapes
    its handlers
and shuffles down to the beach where it stands in the sun for hours.
    It is free
and hungry. An ox lies on the street with three legs tied with rope.
    I'm on another

bottled water run. When I come back, ox is split in strips of meat.
    The vulture
flies home for the weekend. I play placid in conversation and I'm
    agreeable—
you taught me gratitude. A great cavalcade of thank yous to plants,
    animals,

a host with stories about fire-flowers in his childhood village, only
    visible
to those who live without corruption. He says he sees their flames in
    the leaves.
The vulture takes his cousin and me out to a rooftop lounge. I get a
    bout of vertigo.

Try to create space in my body with breaths, but my blood pulls me
    back to the past.
Dance in a bar to Led Zeppelin covers—a whole lotta love for your
    will-o'-the-wisp.
I freeze time for evidence that I've thought of you here, I'm thinking
    of you now.

But never mind. I take the cigars and cognac as they're given. Then he
    drives us
to an empty house and plants stories of secrets and torn-up families.
    *Get in my bed.*
*Don't tell anyone.* How could I? I can't speak. Language has failed but
    I can still run


statistics. One in three Indigenous Canadian women are raped. Women
    in Benin?
One in three. Odds are he hauls me to his bedroom and I play placid
    on repeat.
I brace myself for judgment. Stomach gurgles to digest shame. I
hyperventilate.


What kind of witch possesses the magic to be believed? I hide in my
    locked room
for three days. Watch the shadows of his feet pace under my doorway
    as I plead
stomach ache. I'm a silent captive in this country—what revenant will
    rescue me?

## v. Flight

*You have to tell someone there.* I clutch phone to cheek. Our circumstantial
truce enables your strained voice to counsel me. I choose the priest's son,
who's brought me eggs and mangoes. Usually he laughs with ease. He's
    worried

and decides I'm in danger. At the convent they prepare a ceremony.
    Seven
devotees pray to their divinity while I bathe naked outside in the night,
    washing
away forensic evidence, washing away DEET, washing away mystic
    misfortune

with well water and herbs. Later, the truth lathers even my allies in
    the family.
I brace myself for judgment. Stomach gurgles to digest shame. I
    hyperventilate.
Why-didn't-yous on parade: *I would have fought, I would have screamed—*

*if I were you I would have never been so weak.* I toss in the room the priest's
    wives
have set up for me. Look out on red earth, a lake, palm trees. I force a
    breath—
you taught me gratitude, a great cavalcade of thank yous to plants,
    animals,

the women who bring dried fish and oily sauces and the children who
    beg
for sweets. My stepmom delivers me to a hotel room where I'm
    awakened by
televisions, traffic, power tools and ringtones, or polite knocks and
    whispers.

All send shockwave startles through my body. I send you selfies to
  prove I'm alive.
Freeze time for evidence that I've thought of you here. I'm thinking
  of you now.
You offer to front the four hundred dollars to get my flight changed,
  but my father

mourns with generosity. I medicate with white wine during takeoff
  and turbulence.
Try to create space in my body with breaths, but my blood pulls me
  back to the past.
Replay: I ragdoll, wrist gripped. Clutch the armrest. Sit still. I should
  take up jogging.

## VI. MENDING

Before I left, I sewed a pigskin pouch for your protection. Stuffed it
    with sage
and salt and a lock of my hair. Have either of us ever believed in magic?
The books you've read said we create our own realities. Since it hurt

my fingers to stitch leather to leather, the suffering should fashion
    something.
I'm in this town two months ahead of schedule—slipped timelines.
    Supposed
to come back changed but I hadn't banked on calling Victim Services,
    blood tests,

night sweats. New stained personality refuses to stay with my family.
    Timid
and contrite, I come to yours. Either your mother's kindness or clemency
gets me a rent-free room and I sleep with the stray cats she's collected,
    in spite

of our split and our grief. We don't avoid topics—disappointments,
    apologies, finality.
Both too tired to try again. Still, I cook you dinner and you hold me
    through shaking
fits of depression, cresting PTSD. In the living room of your rented RV

I confide that the sight of my chest contrives nausea and panic. Light of
    electric fireplace
illuminates your hand on my breast. *Is it still okay?* I am warmed
by the question: *Yes.* Days for walking, days when I can't leave my bed.
    All days

I brace myself for judgment. Stomach gurgles to digest shame. I
    hyperventilate.
Try to create space in my body with breaths but my blood pulls me
    back to the past.
You taught me gratitude, with a great cavalcade of thank yous to
    plants, animals,

televisions, traffic, power tools and ringtones, or polite knocks and
    whispers.
I freeze time for evidence that I've thought of you here. I'm thinking
    of you now.
Sigh spells, stitch your ghost back to your body. I commit to the realm
    of the living.

# HERE'S WHAT HAPPENED

On the day of my fourteenth panic attack, I wore a scratchy cream lace dress that flattened my breasts like two upcycled cup coasters. I'm trying to be truthful about having an imaginary friend in high school. How sunlight, the smell of hairspray and my classmates were all too sharp.

On that day, I caught my breath and took the path behind the strip mall, saw the discarded porno mags, blown-out recliners, car tires. Then a shimmering light between two low shrubs. Ovoid, crystalline. I picked my way over some Fruit of the Looms. I touched the light: hand plunged through, came back tingling. The woods were still, but it was a matter of time before some crotch rocket motored by. So I stepped in, right foot first.

I wasn't sure that my foot would hit ground, but the worn grooves of my sneaker found solid purchase. My whole body vibrated as I came over, my vision effervescent, swirling with static and cupcake jimmies. Hands outstretched, I waited. And I saw that on this side, I was the same. The broken bottles and the old hoodies were still scattered about. The sky was grey and low.

The day of my fourteenth panic attack had been ordinary: I awoke alone, let my dog out, wiggled into the thrifted dress. I ate the scrambled egg whites I'd allotted myself. I viciously tore a brush through my hair. And earlier that week, when I'd bothered taking the cramped bus to Math 10, I spent lunch breaks by myself in the washrooms. It was a day like those that came before it and I grounded myself by noting five things I could see, four things I could touch, et cetera.

A portal swallows me at twenty-two, twenty-five, twenty-seven. Sometimes I emerge elegant, slender, teeth bleached white. And I meet the relentless sharpness of each repeating world: there are the same discarded cigarette butts, there's my classmate's cratered arm used up like an ashtray. I dive into these shimmering pools so often I get portal-sick.

This one I've opened myself and my responsibility is not to leave anyone behind. Five things we can see: a modest apartment living room, flattened high-pile carpet, handmade lemongrass lotion from a friend, an antique teapot from a deceased neighbour emanating steam, an abalone shell. It's taking every bit of energy, but can you see the way the world bends to kiss my classmate here?

## STORYTELLING

I dreamt of flossing
my teeth with braids.
Neat plaits wedged
between molars,

scraping out blackberry
seeds. I awoke with a fistful
of feathery hair, soft as a memory.

Plant the skein
in the loose soil
of my fiddle-leaf fig,
make licorice tea,
write lists. My father

told me his mom scraped
the wall near her bed. Gouges
in the drywall. I shake off

the story. Think of rent cheques
and rain. And isn't it too warm?
As if cling wrap was wound
around the apartment,

some savings initiative—
good for the environment—
where we cut little holes
near the windows to stick

arms out and wave to dogs.
Where did I put my spoon?

Stir. Do you know why
I'm afraid of stories lately?

Well, last summer Mom and I
picked blackberries, *plop, plop*
into plastic freezer bags. We stood

in a dirt parking lot. Someone's
liver-spotted spaniel sniffed
brambles, licked up seedy juice.
A coincidence: I had walked
Brownie here years ago,
when I still dyed my hair blue
and dieted. Around that time

my friend gave me the thrift-shop
classic *The Celestine Prophecy*,
which claimed that synchronicities
are evidence of some divine plan.

Like how numbers echo
on digital clocks and song
lyrics crackle like Cassandras
predicting certain relationship
doom via grocery-store speakers.

Mom was playing music
out of her Jeep. Acoustic
songs from a residential

school survivor, his voice
loud as I dropped another
bag of berries off. Hands

stained purple. And I saw
something I shouldn't have seen.
A hole. An eye. Looking.

But what did this eye see?
A woman, her mother,
long hair, berries. Did this setting

satisfy the blond onlooker
locked inside? The dog
barked. The eye squinted,
but never fully shut.

In seventh grade I worried
about the way shadows
framed my face. My best friend
tolerated the proclamations
I made about obsidian omens

shaped like eagles at recess,
hiding under swing sets. She traded
in lies about her absent father
flying her first class to Seattle.

The eagles bled into the world
as I traced their contours. Surely
they would materialize during
my cornered confrontations—

three hollow-boned girls baptizing
me with spit and slurs. The eagles
would save me with some word
or sudden wit, right? Later,

I would recreate everything
with Barbies, finding strength
in the plastic postures, the stiff
countenance. Narrative shift.

*Got a napkin?* My mother waved
her own purple hand from across
the lot. Her berry bag was half
full and torn, juice spilling out

like a wound. I tore three sheets
of paper towel from the roll
nestled between bins filled
with art supplies. *Here,* I said.
Eyes never left the suppuration.

Five years ago my story lived
as a certain disease. Each month
I typed, *Want to die before period?*
Out emerged a narrative
of disorder and curses
and werewolves and inevitability.

I watched moon and tide
with apprehension. Resisted.
Perhaps I was monstrous.
I prowled a six-kilometre radius
around the psych ward.
Snarled, hid in bedsheets,

dreamt of excising
my eggs, swirling

them like pearls
in my mouth,
and swallowing them

like a history
for safekeeping.
A timid man told me
menses are a time of great
connection to Creator. *You're
so powerful right now.*

What a story. I didn't quite
catch his. He built my shelves,
drove me to pick up soil,
bought coffees, laughed.
He held me by a fistful of hair.

I was so sorry for the great
something of my body
that attracts this kind of thing.
Twelve again, and sorry.

Living inside of an apology means:
sorry for limbs, sorry for belly,
sorry for trashing tinned tuna cans,
killing moths, sexual thoughts, striving.

Apology is another kind of story,
sometimes more spackled
than a fable. You know,
like sorry I got caught.
Like, as a nation we are sorry.

The blond onlooker
is a great-grandfather
seeing a great-grandmother
wash her feet by the shore.

They jump rope over the helices
of my cells. She ducks under
his arm and says, *You know
what I don't get?* She twirls.

*I don't get why multigenerational
trauma is seen as one-sided.
As if no one passes damage down
by doing the displacing.* She cites
the article I read about those police

who go home, beat their families,
perpetuating the old generational
double dutch et cetera, like who
are their ancestors?

Great-grandmother invites
great-grandfather to survey
his own scars. To examine his psyche.
What's their history? They go on
dancing for hours, while I buzz sick

and self-centred, believing
I'm a battlefield—it not occurring
to me they've long since made
peace in my bloodstream. We can
talk about agency. Fairy-tale

heroines get done so dirty.
I never think of Cinderella
carving her initials in a tree

or hate-fucking a neighbour,
and whose fault is that?
In her diary she says, *I killed*
*my first stepmom but you all*

*have me clap with songbirds*
*and cry.* Do we seal their fates
in our retellings? Ah, the halcyon
comfort of the wretched worse.

They aren't alone in inheriting
vocabulary. Mine, for instance,
*outcast.* For instance, *loser.*

This Cinderella slipper fits,
shards of glass bound
to me by the heat of nameless
shame. Down to earth
I am not, adjusting the chip
of *crazy* in my footbed.

Mom dab-dabbed her bag
like *there, there.* She folded
the tissues and I stood
by with useless extra.

The music stopped behind us,
a sundog flared. She could just

clutch her chest right now. And me,
I could keep running rampage.

But mom doubled-bagged
her berries. We piled in
the Jeep. We drove off.
We joked. At home we made

blackberry bourbon
jam. The hot syrup
was sticky and sweet.
We danced with spoons

dangling out of our mouths.
We laughed about my sister
dropping a sack of potatoes

and flipping them off in frustration.
About the man who tans
his leathery balls on his balcony.
And about the ludicrous concept

of being unlovable. So that all
of my stories were jarred and jostled,
unprepared to describe my joy.

## ACKNOWLEDGEMENTS

Thank you very much to Silas White, Emma Skagen and everyone at Nightwood Editions.

Versions of poems in this collection have appeared in *Room, The Malahat Review, subTerrain, Arc Poetry Magazine, PRISM International, Adbusters, Soliloquies Anthology, Humanist Perspectives, Transcontinental Ether,* Stuart Ross' project "The Week Shall Inherit the Verse" and Jenya Stashkov's project "15 Canadian Poems."

Some of these pieces were written during the course of my undergraduate degree in creative writing at Vancouver Island University. I would like to offer my heartfelt thanks to Sonnet L'Abbé, whose brilliant mentorship and generous friendship has allowed me to take bigger and bigger creative leaps and has lent me the confidence to settle into my voice. I am grateful to Jay Ruzesky, whose warm support and contagious enthusiasm for poetry helped me feel like I had a place in post-secondary institutions. Thank you to Marilyn Bowering, who suggested, during a time of deep struggle, that I play with different personas as way to access different experiences—the kindness I received planted the seeds for this manuscript and continues to serve me both on and off the page. I am deeply indebted to the care, insights and joy I've received from you all.

Thank you to Stuart Ross for being such a champion of emerging poets. I am grateful for all of the ways you've amplified my work; I am grateful too, for your singular voice and the influence it has had on my poetry.

More gratitude to Liam: you were a first reader for many of these poems and have witnessed their transformations. We've supported each other through a few of our own, and I am humbled to have such an openhearted friend. And Sophie: your authenticity, artistry and incredible altruism has changed me for the better.

Thank you to my many friends who've taken the time to support me and to remind me not to take anything too seriously.

I am grateful to my family. Merci Papa pour m'avoir encouragée tout ce temps et pour avoir lu mes poémes tard les samedis soirs. Merci à Caroline pour le support et pour avoir été une source de stabilité durant une période difficile. Hiy hiy, marci to Mom for keeping the embarrassing clipping of my first published poem I wrote at twelve years old, and of course, for sticking with me through the bisonshit. To my sister Dania: you're the reason I've kept writing at all—thank you for being such an accepting, kind and hilarious friend and sibling. To Brownie, my dear and departed dog sister, thank you for teaching me about personhood.

Thank you to Joseph for loving me throughout all of my shape shifts, for teaching me about presence and unconditional acceptance, and for making me snort-laugh when I least expect it.

## ABOUT THE AUTHOR

Délani Valin is neurodivergent and Métis with Nehiyaw, Saulteaux, French-Canadian and Czech ancestry. She studies for her master's in professional communications at Royal Roads University, and has a Bachelor of Arts in creative writing from Vancouver Island University. Her poetry has been awarded the *Malahat Review*'s Long Poem Prize and *subTerrain*'s Lush Triumphant Award. Her work has appeared in *PRISM International, Adbusters* and *Room*, and in the anthologies *Those Who Make Us* and *Bawaajigan*. She is on the editorial board of *Room* and the *Malahat Review*, and lives on traditional and unceded Snuneymuxw territory (Nanaimo, BC).